THE L

THE LORD'S SUPPER

E. F. KEVAN, B.D., M.TH., PH.D.

EVANGELICAL PRESS

EVANGELICAL PRESS
16/18 High Street, Welwyn, Herts. AL6 9EQ, England.

First published by Evangelical Press 1966
Second impression 1973
Third impression 1982
Fourth impression 1985

ISBN 0 85234 168 7

Printed by Anchor Brendon Ltd., Tiptree, Colchester, Engla

And thus that dark betrayal-night
With the last advent we unite,
By one blest chain of loving rite,
Until He come.

George Rawson.

CONTENTS

PREFACE

To the First Edition

THE following four chapters were originally four addresses given in February, 1960, at Coonoor, South India, to the Conference of Missionaries and Pastors of the Strict Baptist Mission. The author has revised these addresses to a certain degree, in order to make them suitable for reading, but they remain substantially as they were spoken. He would like to express his esteem for the missionaries and pastors who were present, and to thank them both for the opportunity given to him at that time, and now for their courtesy in requesting the publication of them. He would also particularly express his gratitude to his friend, the Rev. D. A. Thrower, for all his labour in preparing this little book for the press.

1. REMEMBRANCE

1. REMEMBRANCE

HOW astonishing it is that we who have been redeemed should even need a reminder! Yet, such is the Lord's understanding of our weakness and the treachery of our hearts, that He has made provision for us to be reminded. It does seem strange that we should forget, but I think if we search our own hearts we shall see that we do need to be reminded.

Luke chapter 22 contains one of the accounts of the institution of the Lord's Supper, and at verse 19 we have the words that we use almost every time at the Lord's Table: "This do, in remembrance of me".

You will know, perhaps, without having to turn them up, that those same words are quoted again by the apostle Paul in 1 Corinthians 11 verses 24 and 25. It is, to me, an inspiring reflection to try to recall the ways in which the servants of God have remembered the Lord's death all down the years. There were the shut doors, at first, in Jerusalem. There was the subsequent meeting from house to house, as they ate with gladness. There were the catacombs in Rome in the times of persecution. Believers all over the world, in times of liberty as well as in times of persecution, have remembered the Lord's death.

The first thing to observe is that this is

1. A commanded remembrance

We have authority for doing this. It is not merely a sentimental arrangement that we have built up, but is ordained by Christ.

It does so happen that the words, "This do in remem-brance of me", are recorded only by Luke and Paul. They probably represent what you might call one line of early tradition. But that does not diminish any of the authority of the words, for if the statement occurs only once in the Bible it has all the authority we want. It is on these words that the permanence of this service of remembrance depends.

Then, further, the fact of the divine ordination of this service is endorsed by the regular practice of the church In Acts 2 we have the account of the first occasion of thei obedience to this command. Verse 42: "They continued stedfastly in the apostles' doctrine and fellowship, and in breaking of bread, and in prayers". Again, in verse 46 "They, continuing daily with one accord in the temple, and breaking bread from house to house, did eat their mea with gladness and singleness of heart, praising God". In Acts 20 we have another insight into the habit of the earl church in this respect, and we learn that it was their custon to meet on the first day of the week. Chapter 20 verse reads: "Upon the first day of the week, when the disciple came together to break bread"; and 1 Corinthians 10 con tains a reference to the Lord's Table in such a way a assumes its regular observance. In chapter 10 verse 1 Paul introduces it as one of those familiar things: "Th cup of blessing which we bless, is it not the communio of the blood of Christ? The bread which we break," (thu referring to the habit of the early church) "is it not th communion of the body of Christ?"

We may also note in passing that the very Greek tens of the word "do" suggests repetition. It was a thing t be done again and again and again. You are familiar wit the words of institution in 1 Corinthians 11 verse 23 an following in which Paul uses the expression, "as often a ye eat this bread, and drink this cup". It would seem from the book of the Acts chapter 2 that they observed the Lord's Table every day. Subsequently, from Acts 20 verse 7, it would appear that it had become by that time a weekly practice on the first day of the week.

The fact that Paul had to deal with abuses of the Lord's Table would seem to imply that the Supper was a well-established practice. In chapter 11 of 1 Corinthians, Paul finds it necessary to rebuke them for the irregularities that attended the eating of the Lord's Supper. Then he goes on to say what it is he is rebuking: "For in eating everyone taketh before other his own supper; and one is hungry, and another is drunken. What? have ye not houses to eat and to drink in? or despise ye the church of God, and shame them that have not? What shall I say to you? Shall I praise you in this? I praise you not". So far as our early church history and tradition give us any light on the matter, it would seem that in Corinth there was a connection between the Lord's Supper and what preceded it in the form of what has been called the "love feast", but there was so little love in Corinth that the rich men sat at one end of the table and ate sumptuously, and the poor man sat at the other end of the table with his meagre fare. There was no communion in this "feast". Then, immediately superimposed on this alleged "love feast" came the observance of the Lord's Supper. The two things contradicted each other. We are not, however, so much concerned with those abuses as with the fact to which those abuses point, namely, that here in the early church it was fully understood that this was a regularly observed remembrance, and that it was by the command of the Lord.

Further, the ordinance was received as a trust. The word that Paul uses when he writes, in verse 23, "I have received of the Lord", is the word that would be used for having accepted a trust from somebody, which, of course would be particularly binding and solemn in its obligations It was a direct word from the Lord that Paul tells us tha he received in this respect. Again, at verse 23, th position of the word "I" in the Greek lays emphasis upo it. It suggests "I, even I, have received from the Lor that which also I delivered unto you". Whether th apostle Paul is referring here to some clear communicatio that the Lord Himself made to him at one time, or whethe he is referring to the fact that he had received this instruc tion through our Lord's disciples, is perhaps not clear but the very fact that he lays emphasis upon the persona pronoun might suggest that in some way the Lord ha especially indicated it to Paul himself. Then the "I, eve I" would be a true representation of the word. The again, "I have received of the *Lord* that which I delivere unto you", indicates that it was authoritative. Thus fro the words of institution and from the practice of the earl church we learn that, when we gather round the Lord' Table from time to time, we meet to do that which we hav been commanded to do. Our observance of the Lord' Supper is by the authority of the Lord Himself.

This might perhaps be the right moment in this serie of biblical studies on the Lord's Supper to notice the term which designate this special remembrance. The greates of these is the one that we have used more than once namely, "the Lord's Supper". This, as you will know is found in 1 Corinthians 11 verse 20. I think there is n better title for this service than this simple and expressiv term. I confess that this is how I like to speak of i in my own pastoral work and in every other connection Here we have the New Testament term.

Just a page or so earlier, and in chapter 10 of this epistle we come across another word for it. It is the wor "communion" (verse 16). The word "communion" is the Greek word *koinonia,* which means "sharing together". The "communion" is joint-participation in the Lord Jesus. I am reminded by this very term that we are not in Christ by ourselves. We are together in Christ, and we share with one another in Christ. The word "communion" in this context does not so much refer to what we might call our upward communion, our direct heart-to-heart participation in the Lord, but our togetherness in Christ. We shall look into this in a little more detail when we consider the word "fellowship" later on. Here, then, is the second word: "the communion". It is a term with which we are familiar in our churches, but perhaps it is one the full weight of which we do not always remember.

Two other brief allusions to the title of this service may be made. In Acts 2 verse 42, it is called "the breaking of bread", and in 1 Corinthians 10 verse 21, it is designated the "Lord's Table". It does not matter which of these terms we use for this service. We may call it the "Lord's Supper"; we may call it the "Breaking of Bread"; we may call it the "Communion"; we may call it the "Lord's Table", and in the use of all these descriptions we shall be correct.

Later on in Christian history the service came to be called "the Eucharist". There is nothing sinister about this particular word: it merely means giving thanks, and reflects the impression that the most characteristic thing about the institution of this ordinance was our Lord's action in giving thanks. And what should elate our hearts more at the Lord's Table than giving thanks? Perhaps we never observe the Lord's Supper so properly as when we lift our hearts in thanksgiving. So, although the word Eucharist has come to be monopolised by certain groups within the Christian church, do not forget its sweet simplicity: it is a thanksgiving.

The chief thing we must not forget, however, is that this thing that we do, we do by command. When we thus gather, we gather not on our own impulse, nor at our own inclination, but because it is ordained that we should do so. Woe to the Christian who neglects the Lord's Table. Unless there are right reasons for being absent, woe to us if we just walk out when the Lord's Table is set. How can we, for some flimsy domestic or social reason, leave the Lord's house when the Lord's Table is spread! How can we turn our back on the Lord's Table! It is an ordinance.

Secondly it is

2. A visible remembrance

Again we see how good the Lord is. The form of this remembrance matches our weakness. We need to *see* things; we want to *handle* things; we are just like Thomas who said, "Except I shall see . . . I will not believe". This kind of remark is not necessarily an expression of terrible unbelief. It is just that instinctive desire for help through the physical senses. The Lord knew all about our need in this way, and so He provided a visible remembrance for us.

The blood that flowed for sin,
In symbol here we see;
And feel the blessed pledge within,
That we are loved of Thee.

Thus, enshrined within visible and tangible objects is the truth of our salvation. It is an external rite, designed by the Lord in His great goodness to impress our senses as well as our spiritual perception.

You will not be unfamiliar with the fact that sacred history is full of such external signs for the bodily senses. Let me remind you of them as I recapitulate them.

When God made His covenant with Noah, He said in effect, "Noah, the next time you see the rainbow" (I do not think this was the first appearance of the rainbow) "remember that that is the chosen sign between us that I will never again destroy the world with a flood" (Genesis 9 verse 17). And every time Noah looked on the rainbow it served as a token to his eye. Then there was the Passover meal itself, with which, as you know, the Lord's Supper has such close affinities. The Passover was something to be observed, and on each occasion, the narration of the Lord's deliverance was to be given as a reminder of what God had done. Again, the Feast of Tabernacles (when the people went out and slept in their leafy huts on the hillside) was a visible reminder of their life in tents and their journey through the wilderness. You will also recall that the rod of Aaron and the pot of manna were laid up in the tabernacle to be a reminder of what the Lord had done. And, finally, by way of examples of external signs, there were the stones of witness that Joshua set up in the Jordan. The stones stood as silent yet eloquent preachers.

The conclusion to be drawn from this, therefore, is that as we think of the Lord's Supper as a visible remembrance, we must take the facts just as they are, and that we must exactly observe this ordinance with its external, visible and tangible signs.

I think it is incumbent upon us to preserve the simplicities of this external service. It is a remarkable thing, is it not, that the objects of the adversary's first attack on the gospel in the course of history have been the two material ordinances, baptism and the Lord's Supper. To corrupt either or both of these obscures, or even obliter ates, the clear outlines of the gospel. I believe that one of the evils in the Christian church today is to be seen in the success which the adversary has had in obscuring the meaning, first of baptism, and then of the Lord's Supper. All the amplifications of the Lord's Supper that almost turn it into idolatrous worship in the church of Rome (and in some other similar communions also) are a destruction of the simplicities that were intended to help the eye and aid the understanding. Let us see to it therefore, that we keep the *simplicity* of the Lord's Table that at the Lord's Table there shall be nothing *less* than has been ordained, but also at the Lord's Table that there be nothing *more*.

What, then, are these elements that are part of the visible remembrance? They are commemorative emblems. "This *is* my body" does not mean identity, as Rome taught, and as Martin Luther refused to give up, but representation. If I hold a photograph in my hand and say, "This is the Queen", you do not understand that piece of cardboard to be the Queen. In the same way, let us remember the liberties that belong to language. I fear that because of our belief in the verbal inspiration of the Bible we often bring a very wooden interpretation to it. Is it not reasonable to understand that the writers of the Bible are using language in the same vivid way in which we use it? Nearly every sentence of ours is shot through with metaphorical expressions, and if we were to be taken up literally in everything we said what embarrassment there would be! Suppose somebody is said to have upset the apple-cart. No one would ask who picked up the apples. Somebody else is said to have sailed through an examination, but no one thinks of enquiring what sort of wind was blowing. Metaphor is in all our speech, and I am convinced that one of the primary needs of the twentieth century is a re-examination of the principles of the interpretation of Scripture.

Here in the words of institution of the Lord's Supper there is obviously an example of metaphorical expression, of the normally vivid way of speaking, which means no more than that this signifies (or this represents) "my body". If you want a piece of convincing argument, as well as the inference to be drawn from the general use of language, you will find it in 1 Corinthians 11 verse 25. Paul reports that "After the same manner also he took the cup, when he had supped, saying, This cup is the new testament in my blood". Now, obviously, the *cup* was not the *covenant*. The cup was the symbol of the covenant: it was the token and expression of the covenant. Further, all materialistic ideas are excluded by the fact that the Supper took place before the Passion and while the Lord was still in His body. The bread and the wine, then, are *signs*, and in themselves they are nothing more. But let us be cautious. This does not mean that the service is nothing more. We are not merely going through meaningless motions. Because the elements, the bread and the wine, are signs, and nothing other, it does not mean that there is not much more in the service. So we come to a third thought. The Lord's Supper is

3. A strengthening remembrance

It cannot but be that the doing of this thing was intended by the Lord to be a means of grace to us. And though it is true that the elements are no more than the signs of our redemption, the ordinance itself is not a *bare* commemoration. I am placing emphasis upon the adjective "bare". I am convinced that what is often called the

Zwinglian view of the Lord's Supper, that is, the com
memorative view of the significance of the elements, is
perfectly correct. But we rise above the elements. The
service is not complete merely in bread and wine. The
active faith of the believer in taking the elements is of
immense significance. He is feeding upon the Lord Jesus
Christ Himself. Thus, while the elements are mere repre
sentations, the service is more than representation. It was
Mr. Spurgeon (if I may hide behind him for orthodoxy
here) who urged his people in one of his sermons on the
Lord's Supper to "feast on Him", and it is this spiritual
reality which is expressed in the familiar Anglican formula
"feed on Him in your hearts by faith". Again, to quote
from Mr. Spurgeon's well-known sermon, "We not only
eat of His bread, but symbolically, we feast upon Him . .
I believe in the real presence of Christ: I do not believe
in the carnal presence of the Romanist. I believe in the
real presence to the believer: but that reality is none the
less real because it is spiritual". How blessed a thing it
has been for you to gather again and again around the
Lord's Table with the Lord's people! Has not it been a
means of grace to you? Has not it been a channel through
which the Lord has shown you His glory and renewed
your faith and sweetened your love? Of course it has
Now, of course, that blessing is not in the elements themselves, but in the service. It is in your believing use of
the elements. Through the believing use of them, your
heart and mind have been lifted up to Him whom they
represent. The confession of faith which was issued from
Zurich under the influence of Zwingli affirmed that "Eating
is believing and believing is eating". You have only to
turn to John's Gospel, chapter 6, for the Lord's authorisation of that interpretation of these things. The Lord's
Supper, therefore, is a strengthening remembrance and

so long as we understand what we mean by that, we may take the full blessedness of that truth.

Perhaps I may sum it up like this: the Lord's Supper is *a special means of grace, but not a means of special grace.* In other words, there is nothing we receive in the Lord's Supper which we do not receive when we are on our knees at home seeking the face of the Lord, or sitting in the pew listening to the preaching from the pulpit. We receive nothing different. The blessing is coming to us through another channel, that is all. There are many means of grace, are there not? There is the means of grace in public preaching of the gospel; the means of grace of the prayer meeting; the means of grace of your own devotional time of private prayer; and there is the means of grace at the Lord's Table. Incidentally, there is also the means of grace in active service. The more you are pouring out, the more the Lord pours in.

But, to press into this even more closely, my next thought is that it is

4. A personal remembrance

There are many things brought to mind in this ordinance. Historically, it was the night in which He was betrayed. "The night"! What a night that was! Just exactly what is the meaning of the Greek word underlying our English word "betrayed" is a little uncertain. The word is *paradosis.* That word, commonly rendered "betrayed", also means "giving up". It is an open question, and stimulating perhaps to your hearts as well as to your minds, to ask whether we are perhaps to understand the word *paradosis* in the sense of "giving up". There were two acts of "giving up" that night. Judas gave Him up: our Lord was betrayed. But, it was also the night in which He gave Himself up. This word *paradosis* is found in Galatians 2 verse 20, where we read, He "loved me and gave himself up for me". You can take the word in both ways and so receive the full significance. It was the night in which He was betrayed, but that was also the night in which the Lord gave Himself up for us in such wondrous love.

This service is also a reminder of the historical basis of our faith. We have to remember that our Christian faith is historically based. In my short journeys in India I had a number of conversations with educated Indian gentlemen, in the aeroplane and in the train, and one of the hardest things I found in these conversations was to get these men to admit the historical basis of our faith. They would say, "everybody has his own ideas about religion". My answer was to confront them with the facts, the historical facts of God incarnate in the Person of Jesus Christ, who lived and suffered under Pontius Pilate. I tried to show them that the saving work of Christ is a thing that can be placed geographically, and can be pin-pointed chronologically. They would then go off again on some philosophical discussion of religious abstractions.

Let us remember that our confidence is not merely the confidence of a book religion; valuable, authoritative, complete and final though this book is. It is in the historical fact of "God, manifest in the flesh".

But the remembrance is far more than the historical one, and by calling it a personal remembrance, I ask your attention to the fact that our Lord said, "This do, in remembrance of me". Our Lord does not ask in remembrance of the date, or the place, but of Himself. Our Lord does not even say: "Do this in remembrance of my death"; although it is perfectly true that the service is full of the meaning of His death. In other words, He says, "Do this in memory of all that *I* am to you". Now, important as is every aspect of our Christian doctrine and every element in the perfect way of our salvation, let us remember that it is not *this* that saves or *something else* that saves; it is *Christ* who saves. Our relation to God is a relation mediated through a living *Person* all the time. It is perfectly understandable when we invite sinners to come to "the cross". But, strictly speaking, we should not do this. If they are not familiar with our evangelical language, they reply, "Well, how can I project myself back 1960 years to something that happened then?" Our gospel invitation is not to invite men to the cross, but to Christ. "Come unto me, all ye that labour and are heavy laden, and *I* will give you rest." "If any man thirst, let him come unto *me*, and drink." That is the true invitation; and so the Lord says, "This do in remembrance of *me*".

You notice that the believers in the New Testament, after they had been observing the Lord's Supper daily, settled down to observe it on the first day of the week—the resurrection day. They did not choose the Friday, the death day. They chose the resurrection day, and by this they have shown us the way to a great truth. The Lord's Supper is a personal remembrance: it is the remembrance of our *living* Lord, whom we know and with whom we have had to do. So, not a doctrine, not a precept, not an event, but a living person is commemorated. We remember not a person who is gone, not a person who was, but a person who *is present*. "For where two or three are gathered together in my name, there am I in the midst of them."

Oh Christ, in Thee my soul has found,
And found in Thee alone,
The peace, the joy I sought so long,
The bliss till now unknown.

Now none but Christ can satisfy,
None other name for me;
There's love, and life and lasting joy,
Lord Jesus, found in Thee.

"This do in remembrance of me." This helps to explain to us whether we are justified in coming to the Lord's Table or not. If you know Him, then of course you can come to the Lord's Table, because you thus remember Him.

My last thought is that it is

5. A spiritual remembrance

The Lord's Supper is not a mere ceremony. It demand the thoughts, the affection and the will. We are remember ing Him in our hearts, not merely observing an outwar ordinance. It is a feast of understanding joy and o dedication.

I did not refer, earlier, to another and somewhat late term for the Lord's Supper that has come to be used i the church, because I think it is probably not a very health one. I refer to the word "sacrament". In itself, the wor sacrament, coming from the Latin *sacramentum*, is perfectly innocent word. It does not mean anythin mysterious. It was the word that was used for the oath the allegiance that the Roman soldier gave to the empero So *sacramentum* thus stood for any sacred and bindin obligation into which a man entered, and in its pure an original sense is a perfectly safe word. Unfortunately is not now safe, because of other connotations which ha been added to it. If we use the word rightly, howeve this name indicates that in the Lord's Supper we obser an ordinance in which the heart goes out and pledg itself afresh in loyal devotion and love. The service accordingly, to be observed as a spiritual remembrance.

This means, first of all, that it will be observed with reverence. In 1 Corinthians 11 verse 27 we read, "Whosoever shall eat this bread, and drink this cup of the Lord, unworthily, shall be guilty of the body and blood of the Lord". What does that stumbling word "unworthily" mean? So many true-hearted believers have been disturbed by a misunderstanding of this. It is said that if you feel ashamed, and crestfallen and depressed because of your failure and sin that therefore you must not come. Oh no! That is the right way to come. To take the Lord's Supper unworthily is to take it without regard to its true *worth.* To do it unworthily is to come complacently, to come light-heartedly, to come without a care about your own sin and your shame. But to be burdened with your sin, even to be weighed down with a sense of your guilt and utter unworthiness—that is to take the Lord's Supper worthily. Only in this spirit do you truly reckon it at its worth.

Let me illustrate this by a lovely incident in the life of Dr. Duncan of Edinburgh. The story is of a communion service at which Dr. Duncan was presiding. In the front pew there was a woman weeping and obviously distressed over her own spiritual state. As the elder was proceeding along the line handing the cup first to one and then to another, this weeping woman shook her head and bade the elder omit her. At once perceiving the spiritual situation, the minister stepped down, gently took the cup from the elder and, stepping back, held it to the woman and said: "Take it, woman, it's for sinners." That is the way to take it. It is for sinners. That is the truly reverent and worthy attitude.

This requires that we shall approach the Lord's Table with self-examination. In 1 Corinthians 11 verse 28, Paul says, "But let a man examine himself, and so let him eat of that bread, and drink of that cup". It is with searching of heart that we must come to the Lord's Table. Let us not come contemptuously or unmindful of the deep solemnities of it. What a searching kind of remembrance this is!

There are some who shrink from the frequent observance of the Lord's Supper. This is not from the fear that it might become unprofitable, but from the fear that it might prove to be too profitable, because this service searches them out and brings the light to bear upon the dark places. Nevertheless, it is possible for us, by the very frequency of our observance of the Lord's Supper, to lose its spiritual significance. Perhaps it is a peril that especially confronts those of us who are committed to the Lord's service as missionaries and pastors. We become so familiar with holy things that they pass us by. We know the words, we know the service. It is a customary service; very often we are responsible for conducting it, and our trouble is that the thing is just going through our head and by-passing our heart altogether. Let us pause, then, and allow the significance of this ordinance to confront us with its demands.

We will remember Him. Do you know the verse by James Montgomery?

> *Remember Thee, and all Thy pains,*
> *And all Thy love to me;*
> *Yes, while a breath, a pulse remains,*
> *Will I remember Thee.*

2. COVENANT

2. COVENANT

N all the four records given to us of the institution of the Lord's Supper we find an allusion to the covenant. urn first of all to Matthew 26 verses 27 and 28. Here, as e Lord is handing the cup after giving thanks, He says His friends, "Drink ye all of it; for this is my blood the new testament, which is shed for many for the mission of sins". You will find identical words in Mark 4 verse 24. So far as we understand the origin of our ospels, the possibility is that there was some written as ell as oral identity between the Gospels of Mark and latthew. There is a slightly different phrasing in Luke 2 verse 20: "Likewise also the cup after supper, saying: his cup is the new testament in my blood, which is shed r you". The meaning, of course, is the same, though e verbal expression is not identical.

The word "testament" in the Bible means "covenant". fact there is only one place (Hebrews 9 verses 15-17) here it seems to be used in the other sense of a man's st will and testament. The word rendered testament normally to be translated "covenant", for it is this venant concept which underlies the biblical use of the ord.

The concept of covenant takes us to the very heart of e historical setting of the Lord's Supper. Its institution as connected with the covenant service of the Israelitish ople of God—the Passover—and we shall not rightly timate the Passover unless we give full allowance in ur thinking to the covenant character of that sacred eal. This being so, it will be helpful for us first of all to spend a little time examining the historical scene which the Lord's Supper is set.

A preliminary question of historical detail thrusts itse upon us at this place. Was our Lord eating the Passov meal in the full and orthodox way, or was He engaged some other sacred meal? The problem is presented to by two passages of Scripture. In Luke 22 verse 15, aft the disciples had gone to make ready the Passover, ar when the hour was come, Jesus sat down and the twel with Him. He says, "With desire I have desired to e this passover with you before I suffer". From that wo it would seem to be perfectly plain that this was the tr Passover meal at which our Lord and His disciples we seated. If you will turn to John's Gospel, chapter 18, yo will find some events which occurred *after* the meal whic Luke has been describing. John 18 verse 28 reads, "The led they Jesus from Caiaphas unto the hall of judgment and it was early (in the morning); and they (the Jew themselves went not into the judgment hall (for it wa Gentile ground and it would be ceremonially unclean them at that time) lest they should be defiled; but that the might eat the passover". Evidently the hour of the Pas over was still to come, so far as these Jewish leaders we concerned, yet in the passage in Luke (and in much of th other evidence of the Gospels) our Lord is said to be pa taking of the true Passover service. All kinds of historic conjectures have been put forward to resolve this appare discrepancy. Some have assumed, though there appea to be no historical evidence for it, that because of th great crowds that gathered at Jerusalem in New Testame times, the authorities had made a special dispensation ar allowed the Passover to be partaken of one day earlie Others have conjectured that when two sabbaths cam together a similar permission was given. But these a only conjectures, and so far as I know, no research into Jewish history in New Testament times has been able to authenticate what would be so very welcome a solution to this particular problem.

I think we must accept two facts. Firstly, that the supper of which our Lord partook *was* the Passover meal. Whatever date it was, and by whatever Jewish permission or special sanction we do not know, but it is quite evident that our Lord was at a genuine Passover meal. Secondly, it is perfectly clear that the Jews were still to eat their Passover meal. The Scripture is quite plain on these two things, irreconcilable though they may appear to be on the surface. Our experience has taught us, however, never to be afraid of what may seem to be irreconcilable things because, as the years have gone by and deeper knowledge has been given, many of the seeming irreconcilables have found their sweetest and simplest solution. For our present study we may accept the fact without hesitation hat the institution of the Lord's Supper occurred during he Passover meal.

Another thing which belongs to the covenant character of the Passover and which will be of fruitful interest to s, is the order of the service. As you know, the meal vas taken in a reclining manner around low tables. There ave been a number of useful booklets about the Passover upper as observed in New Testament times, and you can asily familiarise yourself with the details. But it is ufficient for our present study to note the fact that there vere four cups. There were four formal drinkings of the up at the Passover service. These four cups were interpersed with the eating of bitter herbs, the eating of the amb and of the accompanying bread, and the question y the youngest person of the family present, "What mean e by this service?" (Exodus 12).

Something of this order must surely have characterise
this Passover meal in the upper room with the Lord an
His disciples. An examination of the records would seer
to suggest that the Lord Jesus did not *finish* the Passove
meal proper. Many expositors think that the Lord'
Supper, in its Christian sense, was linked up with th
central portion of the Passover service. The bread th
was eaten with the lamb occurred between the second cu
and the third cup. It was this bread which was dedicate
by the Lord to a new and loftier purpose.

The evidence that it was possibly at this point in tl
order of the Passover service that the Lord instituted H
Supper comes from the fact that the third Passover cu
was called the "cup of blessing", and you will rememb
that this is the phrase that Paul picks up when, writi
to the Corinthians about the Lord's Supper, he asks, "T
cup of blessing which we bless, is it not the communi
of the blood of Christ?"

At this stage in our argument, the record in Luke 22
worthy of a little more attention. The chief portion
from verse 14 to verse 23, and in this account of the Pa
over and the Lord's Supper there is an indication of t
use of two cups. In verse 17 it reads, "He took the c
and gave thanks, and said, Take this, and divide it amo
yourselves"; and then in verse 20, "Likewise also the c
after supper, saying, This cup is the new testament in
blood, which is shed for you". Two cups are h
indicated. Incidentally, there is a difference in the v
that underlies the English here. In verse 17 the word
strictly, He "received" the cup, and it is part of the form
ity of the Passover meal that the second cup be han
to the father who was presiding at the family meal.
shall notice the other word presently.

Here, then, at verse 17, we read that He received

cup that was handed to Him. Probably this was the second of the Passover cups. The Passover order is now followed closely, and there seems no reason to suggest that it is not the ordinary Passover meal proceeding on to the end of verse 18. Possibly at this stage there was a pause in the meal. The meal was a very leisurely one always, taken slowly with a pause for conversation between the eating and drinking. It was possibly in this pause, after the second cup which had been divided among the men, that Judas went out. Undoubtedly, this brought relief to the Lord and the lifting of the load of sadness from His heart.

It is at this point that you may weld the records in Matthew 26 verses 21-25 and John 13 verses 21-30 into this passage. In Luke 22 we have not so much an order of *events* as an order of *thought*. Some of the events, such as the handing of the sop to Judas and his subsequent going out, are described in Matthew 26 and John 13. But now at verse 19 in Luke's record there seems to be a kind of inconspicuous transition into the Lord's Supper. Our Lord takes up the bread which was normally used at this stage in the Passover service and dedicates it to a new purpose. "He took bread, and gave thanks, and brake it, and gave unto them, saying, This is my body which is given for you". The Passover service is now being given a new direction; it is the Lord's Supper.

In verse 20 there occur the words, "Likewise also the cup after supper". The word "likewise" links the Lord's action with His taking of the bread. The word translated "took" is different from the word "received" (verse 17) and implies initiative. Jesus, as it were, takes a step forward. *He* takes the bread and distributes it: *He* takes the cup and institutes it. In this way our Lord transformed the

Passover as He went along in such a manner as to convert it into the Lord's Supper of the new covenant. The Lord's Supper is thus a covenant service.

For an understanding of the full significance of this we must refresh our memories about the two covenants of grace that there are in the Bible. The first of these is called the "old covenant". Do let me remind you that it was a covenant of grace which was made with Abraham, and Paul argues in Galatians that the law which came 400 years afterwards did not alter the character of that covenant. This covenant of grace made with Abraham, and with the people of Israel in him, was, however, under terms of a very limited kind. It is this old covenant that is referred to in Hebrews 9, and we will look at the first verse of that chapter, because it gives us permission to use a certain adjective. It supplies us with the word "first". "Then verily the first covenant had also ordinances of divine service, and a worldly sanctuary."

If I may digress here—I do not think there is any scriptural evidence for what has been theologically called a "covenant of works". You cannot find the covenant of works in the Bible, and even Charles Hodge—one of the greatest of the theologians of last century and a teacher to whom we are deeply indebted—even he says that it can only be "inferred". The Puritans, who had much to say about the covenant of works, all admitted that one could not find the covenant of works in the Bible, but that it was a justly inferable concept. I am not quite so sure, however, that it can be justly inferred in this way. We are told of two covenants in the Scripture. They are two covenants of grace, and one is called the *first*, or old, covenant, and the other is called the "new covenant". The first covenant, given as it was to Abraham and through him to the Lord's people, was ratified in the time of Moses;

and the account of this ratification can be found in Exodus 24 verses 3-8. Moses stood before the people and told them all the words of the Lord. "The people answered with one voice and said, All the words which the Lord hath said will we do." And Moses took the blood and sprinkled it on the people and said: "Behold the blood of the covenant, which the Lord hath made with you concerning all these words". That was the authorisation of the first covenant, but in due time this was followed by the promise of the new covenant. If you will turn to Jeremiah 31 verse 31 you will read, "Behold, the days come, saith the Lord, that I will make a new covenant with the house of Israel, and with the house of Judah". Verse 33: "This shall be the covenant that I will make with the house of Israel; After those days, saith the Lord, I will put my law in their inward parts and write it in their hearts; and I will be their God, and they shall be my people. And they shall teach no more every man his neighbour, and every man his brother, saying, Know the Lord: for they shall all know me, from the least of them unto the greatest of them, saith the Lord: for I will forgive their iniquity, and I will remember their sin no more". That is the new covenant.

But there is something missing here. In the inauguration of the first covenant the terms were first enunciated, and then the blood was shed and sprinkled for its ratification. But there is an incompleteness in Jeremiah's account of the new covenant. The terms of it are enunciated, but it is like a legal document that has not been signed and witnessed. There is no ratifying blood. We have to wait for six long centuries, and then in an upper room Jesus foretells His own death, and as He hands His disciples a cup of remembrance He says: "This is my blood of the new covenant". Then notice how much is included with the additional expression "which is shed for many for the remission of sins".

Those were the terms and promises of the new covenant described by Jeremiah. And so, after the centuries have rolled by, our Lord says in effect, "This is the new covenant, and I am about to ratify it in my own blood". The Lord's Supper is thus the feast of the new covenant, and so far as our enquiry into the historical basis of it is concerned, we may say that it partly accompanied and partly followed the Passover feast. The new was grafted on to the old and the old expired in the new.

May I be permitted to digress. The word "fulfil" which the Lord used about the law and the prophets does not merely mean "come to pass". Coming to pass is only a small element of fulfilment of a prophecy. Fulfilment is as when a bud becomes a blossom, or when the blossom on the fruit tree becomes the fruit. The fruit is the fulfilment of the promise that is in the blossom. So when our Lord said He came to fulfil the prophecies of the Old Testament, we are not to look merely, or only, for external correspondences between a prediction on the one side and an action on the other. Fulfilment is a much richer and deeper concept in which the Lord brings to fruition all that was at first present only in seed and in germ; and so here the old is fulfilled in the new. Our salvation rests in a covenant "ordered in all things and sure".

We will now look into the doctrinal implications of all this. Let us, first of all consider

1. The nature of the covenant

It is described as the "new" covenant. This distinguishes it from the old covenant which, though it was a covenant of grace, was mediated mostly through obedience to law. Even when God made His covenant with Abraham He said: "Walk before me, and be thou perfect". The new covenant is mediated by "the mediator of the new covenant", the Lord Jesus Himself, and the grace that He reveals in His life and death and resurrection. The contrast is stated in John 1 verse 17, where we read, "The law was given by Moses, but grace and truth came by Jesus Christ". These are not violent contradictions, but are complementary methods in God's purpose of dispensing grace. This same contrast is drawn also in Hebrews in a large number of places. Hebrews 8 verse 6 demonstrates the superior ministry of Christ by saying, "Now hath he obtained a more excellent ministry, by how much also he is the mediator of a better covenant, which was established upon better promises. For if that first covenant had been faultless, then should no place have been sought for the second. For finding fault with them (that is, discovering the administrative weaknesses of the first covenant), he saith, Behold, the days come, saith the Lord, when I will make a new covenant". It is something *new*.

Another thing to be observed as we look at the nature of the covenant is that it is utterly and altogether an undertaking of God. All human analogies fail when we try to express divine action, though God has nevertheless taken up many of them, and the concept of the covenant has a limitation in it. Normally a covenant involves two parties, and each party makes a contribution to the effectiveness of it. But in the New Testament covenant of grace there are not, so far as men are concerned, two parties to the covenant. There are within the life of the Godhead two parties—God the Father and the Son, who is the mediator of the covenant, but so far as we who are the recipients of its blessings are concerned, we have no contribution to make at all. This is the place where the concept of covenant breaks down. But we are given a hint of this very truth in the words that the New Testament uses. There are two words for a covenant. One of them has a prefix spelt *sun*, and the other has a prefix spelt *dia*. The word with the prefix *sun* suggests joint action, something that two people do together, and supplies the normal word for a covenant when two men enter into a pledge of this kind. But the Holy Spirit has not used that word when speaking of God's covenant. He has used the second word, with the prefix *dia*, a word which generally suggests something that is laid down or ordained by an authority. The New Testament word for covenant, therefore, is the strong word which excludes the idea of two people or two parties—God and men—making an equal contribution, and reminds us that fundamentally this pledge which binds us to God and God to us is something in which God is laying down all the terms, and in which He also is meeting all the requirements. Thus, although we sometimes speak of the human side of the way of salvation, strictly there is none. Let us think, for a moment, however, of what we mean when we speak of the human side of things in the experience of salvation. You will know, of course, that we mean the empty hand of faith which reaches out to receive the blessing.

Nothing in my hand I bring;
Simply to Thy cross I cling.

Not by works of righteousness that we have done but by His mercy He has saved us. There is a verse in a lovely old hymn which does me much good:

All the fitness He requireth
Is to feel your need of Him;
This He gives you,
'Tis the Spirit's work within.

The new covenant, then, is a divine institution, an undertaking of God combined with a pledge which God gives for the confirmation of it. It used to be said that an Englishman's word is his bond, and I trust that that is still true. So far as God is concerned, His bare word would have been enough, but to meet our weakness, to come to us in the midst of all our fears and tremblings, God, as it were, frames His mercy in terms of a covenant and is pleased to confirm it by His own blood. This covenant is the new covenant.

Yet one more feature of the covenant of grace is that it has for its object the remission of sins. That is what Jeremiah promises, and that is precisely the word that the Lord takes up when He says: "This is my blood . . . which is shed for many for the remission of sins". It is new in the blessings that it gives. For it is impossible that the blood of bulls and goats could take away sins. These were but the shadows of the true, and now the real is here.

Let us now look more closely at

2. The ratification of the covenant

Covenants were sealed in olden days by sacrificial blood. In the present day, of course, if two men want to make a covenant they write out the terms of the covenant and sign it in the presence of a lawyer or other witnesses. But in the old world lawyers were not used for this purpose. Rather, it was a religious sanction that was brought to the agreement. This was the custom before the time of Israel, and it belongs to the whole Semitic world. Look, for example, at the story in Genesis 15, where God makes His covenant with Abraham. God makes the clear promise, but in verse 8 Abraham asks: "Whereby shall I know that I shall inherit it?" In modern parlance he asks, "Where is the trust deed for this? Where is the legal document that makes it sure?" So God says, "Take me an heifer of three years old, and a she goat of three years old, and a ram of three years old, and a turtledove, and a young pigeon. And he took unto him all these, and divided them in the midst, and laid each piece one against another: but the birds divided he not . . . And when the sun was going down, a deep sleep fell upon Abram"; and in the midst of this ceremonial God revealed Himself to him. "Know of a surety," He says, "that thy seed shall be a stranger in a land that is not theirs, and shall serve them." We then read, "It came to pass, that, when the sun went down, and it was dark, behold a smoking furnace, and a burning lamp that passed between those pieces". The flame was an old symbol of the presence of God. "In the same day"—now here is the Hebrew term—"the Lord made a covenant with Abram." The method of making a covenant, as we see it exemplified in this pledge that God made to Abraham, was to "cut" a covenant. The sacrificial offering that was related to the covenant was cut in half and then, if there were two men that were making the covenant, they would both of them walk between the pieces. All this procedure was called cutting a covenant. The sacrificial blood was used ceremonially afterwards in confirmation of it. This is the ratification of an act by means of sacrifice.

We have already observed the presence of sacrificial blood at the Passover and at Sinai in confirmation of the old covenant. Now, here, in the Lord's Supper we come again upon sacrificial blood which ratifies the covenant. The blood is covenant blood. It is not merely blood poured out in affectionate self-giving. It is not merely the blood of Him who loved me. It is the blood of a covenant sacrifice in which God commits Himself in the most solemn way possible.

His oath, His covenant and His blood,
Support me in the whelming flood;
When all around my soul gives way,
He then is all my strength and stay.

We have in the blood of Jesus the ground of our assur-
ıce; a sure covenant, and a ratified pledge to plead.
his is what Jesus meant when He said this is the covenant
n my blood". The little Greek word translated "in"
ıeans "resting upon". In the words of Matthew 26 verse
3, Jesus does not put Himself as inaugurator of the new
ovenant, but rather as the means of its confirmation.
od is the inaugurator of the new covenant. The infinite,
ernal God, the holy Trinity, is the author of it, and the
cond person of the Trinity is the mediator, or the surety,
f it. From this phrase in the Lord's Supper service, a
articularly solemn significance comes to be attached to
e phrase "the blood of Christ". It is quite correct to
peak of the death of Christ, for by this He bore our guilt
way, but we must be careful in this. The death of Christ
nd the blood of Christ are not strictly synonymous terms;
ecause the blood of Christ indicates something more than
e death of Christ. The blood of Christ gathers up into
all the connotation of sacrifice and of covenant and of
uarantee. The blood of Christ is thus one of the most
acred and significant phrases of the gospel, and when some
eople object to the use of the word "blood" in our evan-
elical vocabulary, and say that it is crude and savours of
wer forms of religion, they are completely missing the
ery essence of this truth which comes up to us from the
Old Testament. I hope that none of you will become
ıst New Testament Christians. Remember that there are
ar more words of God in the Old Testament than in the
lew, and do not be believers in just half a Bible. Much

is lost when we speak only of the death of Christ, but wealth of meaning is in the phrase "the blood of Christ"

My blood I thus pour forth He cries,
To cleanse the soul in sin that lies;
In this the covenant is sealed,
And heaven's eternal love revealed.

Having seen the nature of the covenant, and the ratific tion of the covenant, we must now examine

3. The obligation of the covenant

As you know, common meals were of great significan in ancient times. I believe that some Indian ways hospitality are not altogether different from the ancie method in Palestine of spreading a meal.

On these old-time principles, when you have spread meal, and a man has accepted your hospitality, he committed to you and you are committed to him. To e a meal with a man is to "eat salt" with him, and that why you sometimes come across the phrase the "salt of th covenant". To eat salt with a man, to sit at a man's tab and to receive his hospitality, is at the same time to comm yourself never to do any harm to that man. You do n necessarily pledge to him your lifelong companionshi but, having received this hospitality at his table, you woul never be party to any injury or any disloyalty to him. T take a meal, therefore, was at the same time to enter int a pledge. The Lord invites us to His meal, and, in effec says to us, "Come to my table. This is my body and th is my blood. Take this and eat it and drink it, and pledg yourselves to me".

Table-fellowship in this deep sense is to be observed i the Old Testament in Obadiah verse 7: "All the men o thy confederacy have brought thee even to the border the men that were at peace with thee have deceived thee, and prevailed against thee; they that eat thy bread have laid a wound under thee." The sacred loyalties of table-fellowship were being violated. You are familiar, also, with the words of Psalm 41 verse 9: "Yea, mine own familiar friend, in whom I trusted, which did eat of my bread, hath lifted up his heel against me"; that is, "hath made himself strong against me". The thing that made this so awful to the Psalmist was that it was one who had sat at his own table. It was conceivable that Philistines might be against him, but here it was one of his own councillors and friends who had been invited to his own table; that was the poignancy and bitterness of this. Your mind will go at once to John 13 verse 18. Our Lord is speaking about what Judas was going to do, and says, "I speak not of you all: I know whom I have chosen: but that the Scripture may be fulfilled, He that eateth bread with me hath lifted up his heel against me". It was the custom at the Passover feast for the presiding father, if there was an especially honoured guest, to break off a large piece of bread and give it to him first. It was that large piece that Jesus gave to Judas. Then Satan entered into him and he went out and it was dark. The sharp awfulness of Judas's betrayal of Jesus was just this.

All the significance of this comes up in many of the warnings that God gives to His people about partaking in heathen feasts. Take, for example, Exodus 34 verse 15. God is warning them to worship Him alone, "Lest thou make a covenant with the inhabitants of the land, and they go a whoring after their gods, and do sacrifice unto their gods, and one call thee and thou eat of his sacrifice". Numbers 25 verses 2, 3 and 5 refer to this same thing; "And they called the people unto the sacrifice of their gods: and the people did eat, and bowed down to their gods. And Israel joined himself unto Baal-peor; and th anger of the Lord was kindled against Israel . . . An Moses said unto the judges of Israel, Slay ye every on his men that were joined unto Baal-peor". The Psalmis in Psalm 106, refers to this in verse 28: "They joine themselves also unto Baal-peor, and ate the sacrifices c the dead".

Turn over now to the New Testament at 1 Corinthian 10 verses 18 and 21, in the very context of the Lord' Supper: "Behold Israel after the flesh: are not they whic eat of the sacrifices partakers of the altar?" Paul allude here to the fact that for an Israelite to partake in thi sacrifice was at the same time a spiritual recognition of th significance of the altar. He then makes a transition t the thought of participation in a heathen sacrifice. A verse 19 he therefore adds, "What say I then? that the idc is anything or that which is offered in sacrifice to idols i anything?" In other words, nothing happens to the foo by having been offered in a pagan temple. "But," h continues, "I say, that the things which the Gentile sacrifice, they sacrifice to devils, and not to God; and would not that ye should have fellowship with devils.' The meaning of all this is that the table at which you ea is the loyalty to which you are pledged. You cannot ea at the table of devils if you are eating at the same time a the Table of the Lord. Now, my friends, in the grea goodness and mercy of God, the same temptation to ea at the table of devils in the way that was here before thes Gentiles, and might confront many a young convert i India, maybe does not obtain for us at all. But, it is possibl to eat at the devil's table without ever going to a sacrifice It is possible to give your loyalty and your obedience t the adversary instead of to the Lord. It is possible to ea at your own "table", to make a god of yourself, of you own ambition, of your own ministry, and not be a servant of the Lord. In other words, there is an obligation in the covenant, and every time we gather at the Lord's Table we are pledging ourselves in loyalty to Him, whose we are and whom we serve.

In our first study, we noticed the Latin term *sacramentum*, for this holy service. The *sacramentum*, you remember was the pledge that a soldier made to his emperor; and you and I, if we come to the Lord's Table, make our *sacramentum*. We pledge ourselves to Him and to Him alone. I find that the Lord's Table helps me in this way, perhaps more than in any other. It reminds me that I belong to Him and to no-one else.

Here is a last thought:

4. The enjoyment of the covenant

The Lord's Supper is a meal. All down the years, common meals have been occasions of conviviality and of friendship. A feast has been the method from time immemorial for expressing joy. When you have a birthday you have a birthday party; when you get married you have a wedding breakfast. When we want to express our gladness in any matter we have a common meal together, and this is one of the aspects of a meal that the Lord has taken up in His ordinance of the Supper.

You remember that among the offerings that were described in the opening chapters of the book of Leviticus, there was not only the whole burnt-offering, the sin-offering, and the trespass-offering, but there was the peace-offering. In the peace-offering, as distinct from the others, the people, the family, the worshipper, ate the offering. A portion was offered to God to represent the sacrificial character of it, but the peace-offering was essentially a festival meal and all gathered round and partook of it. You will find this described in Leviticus 7 verses 11-15 and Deuteronomy 12 verses 5-7. In the Lord's Supper Christ is shown to be our peace-offering. We enjoy Him as we feed on Him.

Let me remind you that we *eat* the bread, we do not merely *see* it. We do not worship it; we do not merely put it apart; far less do we preserve it, or burn a light by it. We *eat* it. And the cup? We *drink* it. Although our Lord's sermon in John 6 is not a direct reference to the service of the Lord's Supper, it is a divine exposition of our participation in Christ at the Supper. In verse 35 Christ says, "I am the bread of life: he that cometh to me shall never hunger; and he that believeth on me shall never thirst". In verses 51 and 53 and following, "I am the living bread which came down from heaven: if any man eat of this bread, he shall live for ever: and the bread that I will give is my flesh, which I will give for the life of the world . . . Verily, verily, I say unto you, except ye eat the flesh of the Son of man, and drink his blood, ye have no life in you. For my flesh is meat indeed, and my blood is drink indeed. He that eateth my flesh, and drinketh my blood, dwelleth in me, and I in him".

This is the enjoyment of the covenant. "What is the chief end of man?" asks the first question of the catechism. It is "to glorify God and to enjoy Him for ever"; and the Lord's Supper is a feast of joy.

3. FELLOWSHIP

3. FELLOWSHIP

IN this study we connect our thought with the name for the ordinance which is found in 1 Corinthians 10 verse 16. It is the familiar word "communion". It occurs here twice as indicative of the significance of the Lord's Supper: "the communion of the blood of Christ . . . the communion of the body of Christ". Before we are able to see the implications of this for our joy in the Lord's Supper, we must examine the meaning of the word communion as a biblical term. The Greek word is *koinonia.* In the English New Testament *koinonia* is sometimes rendered "communion" and sometimes "fellowship", so that wherever you find either of these words it represents the same word in the Greek New Testament.

I think it will be profitable to approach the word through the use of it. May I remind you again that a word has its meaning, not only by etymology, not merely by definition, but by its use. This is a particularly important principle when we are studying the meaning of biblical words, because a word in the Bible has its own meaning, sometimes quite distinct from its meaning in common speech.

Let us examine the words in Acts 2 verse 42. Here, after the believers had been baptised and were then added to the church, "they continued stedfastly in the apostles' doctrine and fellowship, and in breaking of bread". Here is the word *koinonia.* In 1 Corinthians 1 verse 9, there is another occurrence of the word: "God is faithful, by whom ye were called into the fellowship—the *koinonia*— of his Son Jesus Christ our Lord". Turn to Philippians 2 verse 1, where Paul begins by a series of suppositions: "If there be therefore any consolation in Christ, if any comfort of love, if any fellowship of the Spirit". Before we leave Paul, perhaps we ought to look at some words of his that are more often misquoted than quoted. At the end of the second letter to the Corinthians we find the "benediction". It might perhaps be quite salutary to look at the words in the Bible because very often the quotation of the benediction ends up by reference to strength, companionship, or peace, or any other blessing which the Holy Spirit gives except what actually is written in the benediction itself. It is "The grace of the Lord Jesus Christ, and the love of God, and the communion of the Holy Ghost, be with you all. Amen". Turn now to John's First Epistle, and again your memories will bring back to you the verses that I am going to mention here. 1 John 1 verse 3, reads, "That which we have seen and heard declare we unto you, that ye also may have fellowship with us; and truly our fellowship is with the Father, and with his Son Jesus Christ". Verses 6 and 7 continue the same subject: "If we say that we have fellowship with him, and walk in darkness, we lie, and do not the truth: but if we walk in the light, as he is in the light, we have fellowship one with another, and the blood of Jesus Christ his Son cleanseth us from all sin".

An examination of these and other occurrences of the word fellowship in the New Testament makes it plain that, not only etymologically, but also in its biblical use, the word means a sharing with others in something. It stands for our joint-participation in Christ.

Let us recapitulate for a moment. In Acts 2, the church continued in fellowship: they were together in their joint-participation in the blessings that were in the Lord Jesus Christ. Next, Paul writes to the excessively individualistic Corinthians and tells them that they have been called into the fellowship of His sufferings, into the sharing together in the Lord Jesus Christ. Paul's use of the word in Philippians 2, which belongs to a context in which he is urging them to a unity of mind and purpose, is based on the supposition that there is a "fellowship of the Spirit", and then, in John's First Epistle we have the desire that "ye also may have fellowship with us" and the assurance that "we have fellowship one with another".

What is the blessing which the third member of the benediction brings? We know the grace of the Lord Jesus Christ and all the richness of that. We know the love of God our heavenly Father. But what blessing is it that is particularly singled out for the Spirit in this inspired benediction? There are, as we know, ever so many blessings that come to us through the Holy Spirit, but the one that is named here is that of our fellowship, our togetherness in Christ, by the Spirit. It is rightly called the fellowship of the Spirit because it is the Holy Spirit who creates it. The word fellowship (*koinonia*) was not invented for this purpose: it was found in common Greek speech. But it is instructive to observe that the first appearance of the word fellowship in the pages of the Bible is on the occasion of the giving of the Holy Spirit. When the Spirit came then *koinonia*, fellowship, came, but not before.

One more allusion to the work of the Holy Spirit is important in this connection. Turn to 1 Corinthians 12 verse 13, where I think we have the true key to what is meant by the baptism of the Holy Spirit. "For by one Spirit are we all baptised into one body, whether we be Jews or Gentiles, whether we be bond or free." This teaches that the primary ministry of the Holy Spirit when He came down at Pentecost was to weld the believers, who had until then been so many separate individuals, into the body of Christ, to make them into that living organism which is Christ's body. This, in turn, is the Christian Church itself. If you want a biblical definition of the Church, you will find it here in this very expression. It is nothing other than the fellowship of the Holy Spirit.

You will have seen by this brief study of these occurrences of the word fellowship that it has a horizontal as well as a vertical direction. Very often we speak of communion with the Lord when we mean the blessedness that comes to us in our private prayers, when we are kneeling alone with the Lord and He causes His face to shine upon us. That, of course, is quite true, but it is only half the meaning of the word. It is participation in Christ, but not just that. It is participation in Christ with *others*. So that the biblical concept of fellowship is outward as well as upward.

Before we leave our endeavour to examine the meaning of this concept, let us note in passing the other word that is used in the New Testament for the Church. This is familiar to you all. It is the word *ecclesia,* from which we make up a number of Anglicised words. The word *ecclesia*—a noun—is made up from a verb which has two parts. The first part is the prefix *ek,* meaning "out", and the second part if *kaleo,* the verb "to call". Very often we stop there and say, "Oh yes, that's it; the church is made up of people called out". And that, of course, is perfectly correct. "Come out from among them, and be ye separate, saith the Lord, and touch not the unclean thing; and I will receive you, and will be a Father unto you, and ye shall be my sons and daughters, saith the Lord Almighty". There is truly a calling out.

But that is not all that the word means. In olden days there were no newspapers, and there was no radio. How then was a meeting called in those early days? How were the citizens summoned to a political gathering? This was the task of the town-crier. His duty was to go round the streets and houses of the small Greek city and, after sounding his gong, or making whatever other arresting noise he cared to make, he then announced some meeting at a particular hour at the common meeting place. The verb used to describe the town-crier's function is this word *ek-kaleo,* from which the word *ecclesia* comes. What, then, was the town-crier doing? Was he merely calling them out so that all the citizens would stand at their doors? No! The word that describes his action must therefore mean more than that. The town-crier did not merely call the people out of their houses; he called them together. They were called out together, and that is what the *ecclesia* is. We are not merely called out of sin and out of darkness and out of alienation from God. We are not merely called out of the world, but we are called out together into the company of one another in Christ. If you want another profitable Bible study, go through the book of the Acts and observe the number of times that the word "together" occurs. You can do that quite quickly by using the concordance, but that is a short cut that robs you of a lot of value. What you should do is to find the word in its context and use, and in doing so you will see that the Christian Church is a "together-body".

The word fellowship, or communion, stands for the togetherness of Christian experience. Therefore, when we find in Scripture that the Lord's Supper is called "the communion of the body of Christ" and "the communion of the blood of Christ", the thing we learn is that the Lord's Supper stands as the expression of fellowship.

1. A church ordinance

Here a number of important truths and principles emerge. First of all the Lord's Supper is a church ordinance. We must observe it together. It was an ordinance which the Lord gave to us, His Church, as a Church. We therefore come together to do it. Note the occurrences of this again in the book of the Acts. Acts 2 verse 44: "All that believed were together". Acts 20 verse 7: "Upon the first day of the week, when the disciples came together to break bread". We do not scripturally observe the Lord's Supper unless we come together to do it.

Then again, in Paul's discussion in 1 Corinthians, the same emphases are there (chapter 11 verse 17), although it is in the midst of his rebuke of them for their abuse. Notice the phrase, "Now in this that I declare unto you I praise you not, that ye come together not for the better, but for the worse". So also in verses 18 and 20, "First of all, when ye come together in the church, I hear that there be divisions . . . when ye come together therefore into one place." This was the practice that they were following, namely, to eat the Lord's Supper by coming together. Still again we find in verses 33 and 34, "Where-fore, my brethren, when ye come together to eat, tarry one for another . . . If any man hunger, let him eat a home, that ye come not together unto condemnation". I is obvious from the language of the New Testament tha the Lord's Supper stands as the expression of fellowship and is rightly observed only by believers coming togethe This fact comes out clearly in the word "communion which we are examining.

From all this, it is plain that the Lord's Supper pre supposes the Church. It is an institution that belongs t the company of believers. The primary reference of th Lord's Supper is Christward, as we have seen, and we d this in remembrance of *Him*, but the Scripture also say "Every one that loveth him that begat loveth him also th begotten of him" and, "We know that we have passed om death unto life, because we love the brethren". When was a boy and longing for the assurance of salvation, ne of the passages of comfort that came to me was that erse. I did greatly love the Lord's people. I used to o to our Monday night prayer meeting. Only about ten r a dozen of us met in the little church where I was rought up, and some of the old people prayed long, long, ng prayers! The seats got harder and harder; but in pite of the long prayers and the hardness of the seats, knew I was where I belonged. I knew that here were y best friends and here was my Saviour and Lord, and ne day the light of this just burst upon my longing heart. lthough this was not the foundation of my faith, the asis of my salvation, it was nevertheless one of those uxiliary testimonies that the Lord gave to me in my own eart. Here was an evidence that I had passed from death nto life, because I loved the brethren. You see, I had een brought into the fellowship of the Spirit. I discovered at I belonged to my fellow-believers. The fundamental uth in all this is that we cannot get on without one nother. Fellowship with "the brethren", however, is ependent upon fellowship with Christ. Therefore the ord's Table is for those only who know Christ. God rbid that any should come to His Table who do not now Him. That would be to observe it to condemnation, s Paul says. That would be to observe it unworthily.

The first letter to the Corinthians was written to them check their excessive individualism. One of the results f the quickening grace of the Holy Spirit in the heart of sinner is not only to bring him to God, but to heighten ll his powers. This occasionally creates an excess of dividualism in the believer. By the life-giving Spirit all e powers of personality are intensified, and the believer

is going to be much more a *person* than before he w
born again. The grace of God in us makes us more tru
to be *men*. If we are going to be persons in a fuller wa
then there is going to be more personality and, perhap
in some circumstances—though not necessarily—mo
individuality. This might possibly account for the div
sions and difficulties that appeared in the church at Corin
and which sometimes appear in our own.

With the Corinthians it seems clearly to have been lik
this. They had been brought to acknowledge the Lo
Jesus Christ and, as Paul says in 1 Corinthians 1 verse
the testimony was so confirmed in them that they were n
lacking in any gift. They were simply glistening with gif
but this makes a very difficult community. Perhaps son
of you are praying for that kind of difficulty! You wou
not mind having churches of that sort! They came behi
in no gift but, says Paul in verse 10, "I beseech yo
brethren, by the name of our Lord Jesus Christ, that ye
speak the same thing, and that there be no divisions amo
you; but that ye be perfectly joined together in the san
mind and in the same judgment. For it hath been declar
unto me of you, my brethren, by them which are of t
house of Chloe, that there are contentions among you
It is evident that the Corinthians were showing what mig
be called an excessive individualism, and this excessi
individualism had been carried over into the Lord
Supper. Paul has to rebuke them about this in chapter
They had not rightly estimated the corporate aspect of the
togetherness in Christ. Hence, one of the main burdens
Paul's first letter to the Corinthians is to stress the
togetherness in Christ over against their extreme
individualistic attitude.

Obedience to this ordinance, then, is the joint act
many. It is by coming together in one place and at

ble: it requires our physical coming together. I once
ad a good woman in my first church. She was a kind
nd prayerful person and charming in many ways, but she
ould occasionally be absent for some reason or other.
I saw her, perhaps a few days later, and said "I missed
ou on Sunday", she would normally reply, "I was with
ou in spirit". Our churches are crowded with people
ke that, aren't they? Now, the fellowship of the Spirit
not the same as someone being absent in body but telling
ou that he is with you in spirit. That is not the fellow-
hip of the Spirit in the New Testament sense. Of course,
you are shut away ill in your home and unable to come
the service, then, how true it is that "though sundered
ar, by faith we meet around the common mercy-seat".
ut we must never allow ourselves to forget that the true
ulfilment of the fellowship of the Lord's Supper requires
he joint act of many at one time, in one place, and at
he Lord's Table.

Another aspect of the church-centred meaning of the
ord's Supper is seen in connection with church discipline.
erhaps we should look at two passages here, not to
xpound them but merely to feel the weight of them. In
Corinthians 5, Paul tells them it is commonly reported
hat there is fornication among the members, and of such
sort that even the Gentiles would be ashamed to confess
. In verse 2 he complains, "And ye are puffed up, and
ave not rather mourned, that he that hath done this deed
night be taken away from among you. For I verily, as
bsent in body, but present in spirit, have judged already,
s though I were present, concerning him that hath so
one this deed". Now these are the instructions: "In
he name of our Lord Jesus Christ, when ye are gathered
ogether, and my spirit, with the power of our Lord Jesus
hrist, to deliver such a one unto Satan for the destruction

of the flesh, that the spirit may be saved in the day of t
Lord Jesus". Here is an important and solemn paragra
on church discipline. It would be unfair not to make a
comment on verse 5: "Deliver such a one unto Satan f
the destruction of the flesh, that the spirit may be saved
These words might have two meanings. First, you a
either the Lord's, or you are Satan's. You are either
the Lord's side, or you are on the devil's side, and Pa
envisages someone professing to be on the Lord's si
who is attempting to come to the Lord's Table, yet w
really belongs to Satan. Therefore, says Paul, put h
away to where he belongs, that is, outside the fellowsh
of those who are on the Lord's side. A second possib
explanation might be that here (by a special inspirati
that the Holy Spirit was giving to Paul at this time) he w
saying that God in His mysterious providence sometim
allows one of His children to be put in Satan's sieve. T
Lord allowed Job to be in Satan's hand, and permitt
Simon to be put into Satan's sieve similarly. Satan
God's servant at every turn, and it may be that in Corin
God was allowing these believers to be put into t
sifting, testing power of Satan for the saving of the spir
Either of these meanings may belong to the words of ver
5, but the burden of what Paul is saying to the Corinthia
is that the fellowship of the Lord's Table requires that a
those whose conduct is openly contradictory to that f
which the Table stands, must be put out of the fellowshi

The apostle writes in the same way to the Thessalonia
in 2 Thessalonians 3 verse 6: "Now we command yo
brethren, in the name of our Lord Jesus Christ, that
withdraw yourselves from every brother that walketh di
orderly, and not after the tradition which he received of u
For yourselves know how ye ought to follow us". He
again, is an instruction from the apostle Paul to exerci

urch discipline, because the fellowship of the Lord's
ıble must not be marred. In this latter passage, the man
ıo walks disorderly is still a *brother*. This implies that
: do not have to make some verdict about the eternal
stiny of those who stumble. Discipline is for the preser-
tion of the purity of the fellowship, and there is a close
nnection between church discipline and the Lord's
pper. The erring brother in this respect is excluded
r the time being from church fellowship. The act of
communication, or whatever word you care to give it,
plies nothing if it does not imply exclusion from the
ord's Table. If the Supper is simply the private com-
union of the individual and God, then the church has no
ht to exclude anybody from it. But since it is not
erely the private relation between the individual and
od, since it is horizontal and binds us together, then, of
urse, such discipline must be exercised, and the signifi-
nce of the ordinance is to be understood accordingly.

Perhaps one short observation is not out of place here.
has to do with the taking of the Communion Service to
e bedside of a person in hospital or in his home, or what
sometimes called a private communion. In the early
ys, our Protestant forefathers strongly resisted this, and
e reason was obvious. The Roman church and, in some
easure, other churches, had completely abused the Lord's
pper and had turned it into an administration in which
e one who dispensed it assumed the function of a priest.
e came to the sick man in his bed and, as it were, "did"
mething to him. Now that is a complete denial, an
solute cutting at the roots, of the significance of the
ord's Supper. There is nothing unscriptural, however, about
e observance of the Lord's Supper around the bed of a
ck man provided the biblical pattern of the Lord's Sup-
r be preserved at such an observance. This means that

the minister is to bring around the bed a company of t
church in miniature. It should never be just the si
person and the minister, for then an utterly false relati
comes almost unconsciously to be created. Let the elde
of the church be present; let there be two or three believe
together with the minister. If all these cannot assemb
then let there be at least just one more, together with t
minister and the sufferer. This provides what we read
in Matthew 18 verse 20: "For where two or three a
gathered together in my name, there am I in the midst
them". I hope I am not unkind here, but I cannot he
feeling that the requests that we ministers occasional
receive from people in hospital are sometimes inspir
by a superstitious idea about the Lord's Supper that th
have learned from their neighbours. I do neverthele
appreciate that some bed-ridden saint of God who h
been cut off from the joys of the house of God for ma
a long month would greatly rejoice to be able to rememb
the Lord's death with his fellow-believers in a gatheri
of them in his room or in the hospital ward. What
desire to say here is that I think we must be cautious abo
our use of the Lord's Supper in our ministry to the sic
we must be watchful lest we countenance some erroneo
conception of it.

2. The nature of the Church

Secondly, the fellowship of the Lord's Table defines t
nature of the Church. Because the Lord's Supper is
fellowship, it defines the nature of the Church in terms
the *equality* of all its members. "All ye are brethren
The participants in the Lord's Supper sit around the Tab
It used to be the beautiful custom in the Anglican chur
about four centuries ago that the Communion Table was
the centre of the building and all the seats and pews we

:ranged around it. That had certain inconveniences from ıe point of view of the preaching and eventually the Table as moved to the end, but the symbolism of the Table is ıat the pastor and deacons are around the Table together ith the congregation. Here is our equality. The fellowıip of the Lord's Table symbolises the mutual regard ıat we have for one another and for the Head.

The Lord's Supper also reveals our equal *dependence* pon Christ. We all eat, we all drink, we all need the ıme nourishment from the Lord Lesus. I just remind ɔu, without asking you to turn back to it, of the passage ıat we noticed in the Gospel of John about the eating and rinking of the body and blood of the Lord Jesus. As read nourishes, so feeding upon Christ nourishes and ıstains the life, and every time we come together to the ord's Table we are making an outward acknowledgment ıat we live by Him, that He is our nourishment, that He ; our strength, and without Him we fade away. If we ıay contrast the ordinances of baptism and the Lord's upper, we can say that baptism symbolises that we are ı Christ and the Lord's Supper symbolises that Christ is ı us.

But further, the fellowship of the Lord's Table defines he nature of the Church not only in the equality of its ıembers and their common dependence on the Lord, but lso in its *unity*. The Table is a means of uniting a conregation, in binding the believers in common loyalty. Each individual identifies himself with the next as he sits y his side. Paul's expression in 1 Corinthians 10 verse 7, is significant here. He writes, "For we being many are ne bread, and one body: for we are all partakers of that ne bread". This is Paul's exposition of his previous emark in which he has asked of the cup of blessing which ve bless "Is it not the communion of the blood of Christ?

The bread which we break is it not the communion of t
body of Christ?" We often think of ourselves as "bei
many" when we are away in our homes, or away in o
factories or in our shops. We are isolated and lonely, b
at the Lord's Table we "being many" are one bread a
one body, for we are all partakers of that "one bread".
chapter 11 verse 29, Paul deals with the possibility of tho
who eat and drink unworthily, and, you will rememb
this means eating and drinking without regard to the wo
of the ordinance. The feature of their wrong behavio
on which he fastens is that they are "not discerning t
Lord's body". In the first place, this means the body
the Lord Jesus that was given up in death: we mu
discern that in the Lord's Supper. But secondly, a
growing out from this, is the spiritual body, the Churc
because that is what Paul has been describing in the pr
vious chapter. We are one body, and a failure rightly
observe the Lord's Supper is a failure likewise to recogni
the unity of believers in their common life in the body
Christ.

Ephesians 5 verse 30 stresses this truth and so also do
1 Corinthians 12 where, as you know, Paul uses the figu
of the human body as a picture of the Church. "T
supper," said John Smythe, one of the Baptist pioneers
the year 1610, "is eaten only by those who are flesh of H
flesh and bone of His bone in the communion of the Ho
Spirit." At the Lord's Table there is demonstrated
the most solemn and impressive manner that we belo
to one another. Paul exclaims about one company
Christians, that they did better than he had hoped. Is
it grand when in a pastorate your believers do better th
you are expecting of them? He explains that "they fi
gave their own selves to the Lord, and unto us by the w
of God". At the Lord's Table we are giving ourselves

one another. There is a little proverb which is full of meaning, which runs like this: "A man who is wrapped up in himself makes a very small parcel". How many of us are wrapped up in ourselves! We are thinking of our own spiritual prosperity; we are thinking of our own spiritual comfort; or we are thinking of our own eternal hope, of our own sins, or of our own this and that. If only we would *give* ourselves; if only we would commit ourselves not only to the Lord but to one another! That is what the Table does. How many of us bring ourselves into condemnation through not appreciating the reality of the Lord's body! Let us unite ourselves around the Lord's Table.

Now I know the doctrinal importance of preserving the Lord's Supper and preserving the church order which the New Testament teaches in the relation of baptism to the Lord's Supper, but there are some differences that we must sink in the presence of the Lord's Supper as fellowship. Mr. Spurgeon once made the remark: "I know many a brother with whom I cannot agree on certain points, but I can agree with him in remembering the Lord Jesus. I could not work with him in all he does, but if he wants to remember the Lord Jesus I can join him in that". I do not quote this in any way of controversy, but what a good thing it would be if we could triumph over the barriers that come between fellow-believers. Some of these barriers have no reality in them, yet we allow them to cut us off from one another.

Then, finally, the Lord's Supper as fellowship teaches us

3. The holiness of the Church

This is never more clearly seen than at the Lord's Table. If the things that are symbolised at the Lord's Supper

stand for anything, they stand for things that are inca
descently holy. I confess that I find no fault whatev
with the Anglican description of the Lord's Table as th
"holy table". Biblically, the title is the Lord's Tabl
but by inference the Lord's Table is a holy table. "L
a man examine himself" as he comes to this Table. Th
very requirement of examination and heart-searchin
demonstrates the holiness of the Table, and therefore th
holiness of the fellowship that meets around it.

Let us resolve to keep the unity of the Spirit and s
make good the fellowship. Are you keeping fellowshi
with your fellow-believers? Are you keeping in fellow
ship with your brother, pastor, and other church members
Are you holding yourself aloof, or are you giving yourself

Allow me to finish by telling you this beautiful stor
He was a good man but, like many another good ma
he had been tripped up. Something had happened in th
church that upset him, and so he stayed away. He wa
denying "the fellowship of the Holy Spirit". He wa
absenting himself from the worship and from the Lord'
Table. The pastor went to see him, and after they ha
talked over the issues involved, as they were sitting by a
open fire, the pastor took the tongs from the hearth an
separated the flaming coals and spread them around th
outer circumference of the open grate. In a few moment
the flames died down, and in another few minutes th
coals lost their brightness and grew ashen and dull. Th
pastor looked at his member and said, "Do you under
stand?" The man had grace and wisdom enough to say
"Yes, pastor, I understand". Then he took the tong
again and, taking the coals from the outer edge of th
grate, he drew them all together; and you know wha
happened. They had not been together many moment
before they began to glow once more. Then they cam

up in flames and the fire was strong. Again the pastor looked at his erring member and said, "Do you understand?" Do you? Let nothing divide you in your fellowship with your fellow-believer, because you will both be the losers. Not only will you both be the losers, but so will the integrity of the church: the flame will go down, and the fires of revival will depart. We are together in Him, and the Lord's Supper draws us together. The nearer we are to the Lord at His Table the nearer we must be to one another. Keep the fellowship real.

In Hebrews 10 verse 25, we are provided with an insight into the early church. It seems that even in New Testament days people belonged to the Church in order to stay away from it. In this letter the apostle says, "Not forsaking the assembling of yourselves together, as the manner of some is; but exhorting one another: and so much the more, as ye see the day approaching". Let us take heed to this warning.

4. HOPE

4. HOPE

THE Lord's Table around which we gather as Christians from time to time is, as we have seen, first of all, a place at which we remember Him. It is also the sign of God's pledge, God's covenant to us in the precious blood of Christ. The Lord's Table is also the centre of our spiritual fellowship one with another in Christ. But I want us to think of the Lord's Supper now as the service of hope.

There is something forward-looking in the Lord's Supper, and it is this hope that I want you to catch. Have you ever said goodbye to somebody with the sinking feeling in your heart that you would never see them again? But if there has been the faintest hope that you would see them once more, that there would be some opportunity of being reunited, well, what a difference that has made! The Lord left His disciples and He went up where He was before. But His going away was not the end of hope, it was not the beginning of depression; because concerning Him there was not merely the faint hope, but the clearest teaching that He would come again. The Lord's Supper, looking not only backwards to the cross, but also forward to the second coming of the Lord Jesus Christ, is the token and constant witness to the fact that the Lord Jesus is to return and that before us there stretches out a vast prospect of glorious hope. The Lord's Supper is the token of the Lord's return.

Look now at the First Epistle to the Corinthians, for example, in chapter 11. At the end of the words which describe the institution of this Supper we have words like these: "For as often as ye eat this bread, and drink

this cup, ye do show the Lord's death till he come". "Ti
He come." The Lord's Supper every time says to us, "H
is coming back". This is not a perpetual observanc

There is to come a glorious moment when it will b
consummated and realised in glory that is unspeakabl
in an intimacy of face to face union with God which w
have never imagined down here. It is to be observe
"till He come". The Lord's Supper then, is a servic
of *hope*.

Not only is this hope clearly stated in words like thes
in Paul's letter, but there are features about the institutio
of the Lord's Supper which build up to this great expecta
tion. Turn to the words of Matthew 26 verse 29. Th
previous verses describe the institution of this service, an
then our Lord says, "But I say unto you, I will not drin
henceforth of this fruit of the vine, until that day whe
I drink it new with you in my Father's kingdom". This
or course, is the same truth which is recorded in Luke 2
verses 16 and 18, where our Lord has described His grea
desire to eat this Passover, and adds, "For I say unto you
I will not any more eat thereof, until it be fulfilled in th
kingdom of God. . . . For I say unto you, I will not drin
of the fruit of the vine, until the kingdom of God sha
come". These words, recorded by Matthew and Luke
link the Lord's Supper with other teachings of our Lord t
the effect that they are onward and forward-looking i
direction. For example, turn to chapter 14 verse 15, o
Luke's Gospel. In the middle of a conversation wit
Jesus about a great supper, when "one of them that sa
with him heard these things, he said unto him, Blesse
is he that shall eat bread in the kingdom of God". I
other words, in Jewish thought of New Testament times
the annual Passover meal pointed on to the consummatio
of things which was regularly described in Jewish writing

and preaching as a Messianic feast. Again and again the Jews described the glorious blessing of Messiah's advent in terms of a banquet. It is no wonder this very superficial, but possibly quite devout, person said, "Blessed is he that shall eat bread in the kingdom of God".

This will, doubtless, bring to your mind a number of the parables spoken by the Lord Jesus, and other allusions to the glorious end of things in terms of a feast, or banquet. You remember the story of the wise and the foolish virgins. In this parable it was a matter of entering into a wedding feast, and those who were ready went in, but those who were not wise and not ready were excluded. Then you will recall that our Lord tells a story of a king who made a wedding feast for his son, to which many people were invited. Those who were invited declined to come, and so the king sent the message to all and sundry to come in and, as they entered, they were given the wedding garment. Our Lord regularly described the things that were to come in the figure of speech which Jewish expectation already provided in terms of a banquet. Listen to the words that Jesus spoke about servants who are faithful. In Luke 12 verse 37, He urges His followers to be like men who wait for their Lord, and says, "Blessed are those servants, whom the Lord when he comes shall find watching: verily I say unto you, that he shall gird himself, and make them to sit down to meat". Again, speaking to the argumentative Jews in the next chapter (Luke 13 verse 28), He says, "There shall be weeping and gnashing of teeth, when ye shall see Abraham, and Isaac, and Jacob, and all the prophets, in the kingdom of God, and you yourselves thrust out. And they shall come from the east, and from the west, and from the north, and from the south, and shall sit down in the kingdom of God. And behold, there are last which shall be first, and there are first which shall be last". The religious people of His day would be kept at a distance, but those who were humble enough to be followers of the Lord Jesus would be at the banquet. Listen once more to what our Lord says to His disciples in Luke 22 verses 29, 30: "And I appoint unto you a kingdom, as my Father hath appointed unto me; that ye may eat and drink at my table in my kingdom". The last passage to which I would like you to turn is in the last book of the Bible (Revelation 19 verse 9): "And he saith unto me, Write, Blessed are they which are called unto the marriage supper of the Lamb". Thus, when our Lord chose in His sovereignty to keep His disciples reminded of Him by the institution of a feast, He was building not only on the past, that is to say, the Passover feast; He was also building on the expectation that was in every godly Jewish heart that Messiah's glory and His vindication would be expressed in the form of a wondrous banquet. The Lord's Supper is, therefore, anticipatory: it points beyond itself to something bigger than itself. In fact, the Lord's Supper is always saying, "Till He come"; "Till He come".

Feast after feast thus comes and passes by,
Yet passing, points to the glad feast above,
Giving sweet foretaste of the festal joy,
The Lamb's great bridal feast of bliss and love.

In the light of this, we must endeavour to receive to ourselves the meaning and the purpose of this forward look in the Lord's Supper. First of all, the Lord's return is an event which may be anticipated with

1. Certainty

We do not properly observe the Lord's Supper unless we accept the truth of our Lord's return. It is a one-sided use of the Supper merely to look back to the cross; we must also look on to the crown. Let us, therefore, believe this truth of the Lord's return.

But this is not the same as accepting certain schemes of prophetic interpretation. May I plead for a spirit of brotherly tolerance in matters of interpretation. In the wisdom of God, there seems to be some holy purpose that He may have in leaving us to our hard thinking on this, while not yet being able to come to any clear definition of the time and manner of our Lord's coming again. But we must accept the truth of a personal return of the Lord Jesus Christ, because the plain teaching of Scripture is that He who came to the earth in the lowly manger will come again in the clouds of glory. This is what we mean by the second advent.

The world did not see the last of Jesus when it crucified Him and buried Him in the ground. The cross was followed by the resurrection, the ascension, and the enthronement of Christ at the right hand of the majesty of God on high, from whence He will come to judge the living and the dead. "Behold he cometh with clouds; and every eye shall see him." Jesus made this perfectly plain in John 14 verse 3. Talking in intimacy with His disciples, He said: "I will come again", and the parables of the Lord Jesus point in the same direction. We have, further, the words that were spoken to the disciples as they looked up into heaven as Jesus was taken from them. "Behold, two men stood by them in white apparel; which also said, Ye men of Galilee, why stand ye gazing up into heaven? This same Jesus (and the force of that expression is 'Jesus His very self') which is taken up from you into heaven, shall so come in like manner as ye have seen him go into heaven." Another passage that always kindles our Christian hearts is 1 Thessalonians 4 verse 15. "This we say unto you by the word of the Lord, that we which are alive and remain unto the coming of the Lord shall not prevent them which are asleep. For the Lord himself shall descend from heaven with a shout, with a voice of the archangel, and with the trump of God: and the dead in Christ shall rise first: then we which are alive and remain shall be caught up together with them in the clouds to meet the Lord in the air: and so shall we ever be with the Lord. Wherefore comfort one another with these words." Let us acknowledge this truth.

But secondly, by this Supper the Lord's return is presented as a joyous

2. Prospect

The Lord's Supper keeps fresh in our minds the expectation that He will come again. Every time the church gathers round the Lord's Table there rings out from that Table the cry, "Even so, come, Lord Jesus". The Lord's return is the great hope of the Church; it is something for us to cherish, something for us to hug to our hearts amid all the difficulties, adversities and frustrations of the present day. Let us cherish it warmly, "Looking for that blessed hope, and the glorious appearing of the great God and our saviour Jesus Christ" (Titus 2 verse 13); and "Looking for and hasting unto the coming of the day of God" (2 Peter 3 verse 12). "Unto them that look for him", says the writer to the Hebrews (9, verse 28) "shall he appear the second time without sin unto salvation." That is the happy attitude of expectant belief and, my brothers and sisters, as surely as you and I take our stand beneath the cross of Jesus so we may lift up our eyes to the coming of Jesus, because one belongs to the other. The second coming is but the consummation of the cross

The real victory was at the cross, and its implementing is in His coming.

The hope which the Lord's Supper enshrines challenges us to maintain constant

3. Vigilance

It is not impossible for the spirit of scepticism and rejection of this truth to settle down upon our spirits. You remember those words in 2 Peter 3 verses 3 and 4: "Knowing this first, that there shall come in the last days scoffers, walking after their own lusts". Incidentally, that phrase explains the previous one, for people scoff at this truth only because they want to indulge themselves. They say: "Where is the promise of His coming? for since the fathers fell asleep, all things continue as they were from the beginning of the creation". But the word of the Lord is, "Watch". "Be ye also ready; for in such an hour as ye think not the Son of man cometh." There is need for spiritual vigilance as we cherish the thought of our Lord's return.

I wonder, whether, by any chance, the truth of the second coming of the Lord is a disturbing thought to you. I wonder whether all this fills you with a sense of dismay and dread. It need not fill you with anything like that at all if you know Him. It might well fill you with fear and dread, however, if you do not know Him; because when the Lord Jesus comes back it will be to judge the living and the dead. But those who belong to Him, those who love Him, are safe in His keeping. It is only those who love their sins, who cannot welcome the thought of the return of the Lord Jesus; but if you hate your sins and love the Saviour, then the prospect of His return can bring you nothing but comfort, peace, and rest in your heart.

Fourthly, the Lord's Supper supplies us with a deep and strengthening

4. Consolation

What a consolation this Supper brings to us in its forward-looking hope!

When the weary ones we love
Enter on their rest above,
Seems the earth so poor and vast,
All our life-joy overcast?
Hush, be every murmur dumb;
It is only till He come.

What a gathering and rejoicing there will be when He comes! We take to heart the triumphant words of 1 Corinthians 15 verses 19-23: "If in this life only we have hope in Christ, we are of all men most miserable. But now is Christ risen from the dead, and become the first-fruits of them that slept. For since by man came death, by man came also the resurrection of the dead. For as in Adam all die, even so in Christ shall all be made alive. But every man in his own order: Christ the first-fruits; afterward they that are Christ's at his coming".

Friends will be there I have loved long ago;
Joy like a river around me will flow;
Yet, just a smile from my Saviour, I know,
Will through the ages be glory for me.

God will bring them with Him. Let us see to it that our hope is in Him, in the risen Lord who is returning, and then all the comforts of God about those who have fallen asleep in Jesus will come to us. I do not know how often some of you may have had to gather for a funeral service. It often happens that the coffin is brought in and placed just where the Table normally stands. Let this coinciding of place draw your eyes away from the grave and into the glory, passing from the body to the thought of the one who is now present with the Lord and whom you will meet again "with Him". No wonder Paul said: "Comfort one another with these words".

In the fifth place the upward and forward-looking emphasis of the Lord's Supper points to a

5. Purpose

Our Lord went away in fulfilment of a purpose. He is now seated and enthroned. "Wherefore he is able also to save them to the uttermost that come unto God by him, seeing he ever liveth to make intercession for them" (Hebrews 7 verse 25).

The "till He come" of the Supper reminds us that although He is away, He is nevertheless occupied on our behalf.

'Tis He, instead of me, is seen,
When I approach to God.

Further, exalted and reigning as He now is, it is He, said Peter, who has shed forth the mighty influence in the coming of the Holy Spirit. Let us remember then, as our eyes are lifted heavenward, that our Lord is on the throne and exercising His own sovereignty now; and when He returns it will be but to gather up the results of His own working during all these intervening centuries.

Finally, we remind ourselves that the hope inspired by the Lord's Supper is not without its

6. Demands

These demands meet us on two sides. There is the demand, first of all, for *suitable conduct*. This is what Peter says when, speaking of the day of the Lord that will come as a thief in the night, in which the heavens shall pass away with a great noise and the elements shall melt with fervent heat, he urges, "seeing then that all these things shall be dissolved, what manner of persons ought ye to be in all holy conversation and godliness, looking for and hasting unto the coming of the day of God" (2 Peter 3 verse 11). If we turn over a page and come to 1 John 2 verse 28, we find the aged apostle saying, "Now, little children, abide in him; that, when he shall appear, we may have confidence, and not be ashamed before him at his coming". Oh, my brothers and sisters in Christ, let us seek to live today in such a way that, when we have to give an account of this day in His presence and at His coming, we shall not be ashamed. In the next chapter of this delightful letter (1 John 3 verses 2 and 3) John says, "Beloved, now are we the sons of God, and it doth not yet appear what we shall be: but we know that, when he shall appear, we shall be like him; for we shall see him as he is". Now that is glorious, isn't it? When He appears our very sight of Him will transform us into His likeness. But that is not all that John says. He adds that because of this prospect, "every man that hath this hope in him purifieth himself, even as he is pure".

You will know, as most thoughtful Christians know, that the discussion of the details of the Lord's return has sometimes provoked dissension and controversy in the hearts of very good people, but the purpose of this "hope" that we have in Him is that we shall purify ourselves even as He is pure. This is the spiritual purpose of our hope in Christ, and it is written large for us in the Lord's Table.

The second aspect of this demand is for *suitable service.* Two of our Lord's parables about His return were connected with service; they were concerned with what His faithful servants must do and be. You remember the parable of the talents. This parable lays stress upon the faithfulness of the servants. One man had five talents, one had two, and another had one. The man who had five was expected to produce five. The man who had two was not expected to produce five, but he was praised because he had produced two. This means that the Lord expects faithfulness according to the gifts He has bestowed. This parable, therefore, emphasises fidelity. But take the parable of the pounds. They all had one pound each: all ten of them. But one of them had gained ten pounds, and another had gained five. They were commended this time for their industry. God wants both these things from us. He expects our utter fidelity in using the gifts He has bestowed upon us and their full deployment in the Lord's service; and He also expects our industry in putting into the Lord's work all the vigour and strength that God has entrusted to us. How great will be the privilege of receiving the Lord's "Well done" in respect of both our faithfulness and our industry!

"Occupy," says the Lord in the parable, "till I come." When the Lord comes there will be unexpected rewards. It is possible that there will be inversions, too. I sometimes think of missionaries and preachers who have a kind of glamour round them; but it may well be that in the great rewarding day some of those whose names have never been known in the Christian Church, some of those who have never occupied the pulpit; some who have never sung a solo, or have never played the organ, who have never even given out the hymn books, or done anything that anybody has noticed, will receive a major award. If there has been in their hearts an utter faithfulness in the use of the talent that they were given, and if there has been painstaking industry in their service, it could easily come about that some of the unknown people will receive a greater reward than others of us who have been in the public eye.

Listen to Paul as he writes to the Thessalonians. As he thinks about them, among the firstfruits of his labours, he says (1 Thessalonians 2 verse 19): "For what is our hope, or joy, or crown of rejoicing? Are not even ye in the presence of our Lord Jesus Christ at his coming?" It was Samuel Rutherford who said, "My heaven will be two heavens, to see you there". It is you who work for the Lord in your various spheres in the churches, the schools, and in the mission field to whom this encouragement belongs. What a joy, what a crown of rejoicing, it will be when you find some poor old woman; when you find some sinful old man who has been brought to know the Lord; when you find some young boy or girl whom you were able to lead to Christ; when you find these "around the throne of God in heaven". That is going to be your reward. That is going to be your crown of rejoicing, and it is part of the "hope" to which the Lord's Supper points.

"I have fought a good fight, I have finished my course, I have kept the faith; henceforth there is laid up for me a crown of righteousness, which the Lord, the righteous Judge, shall give me at that day: and not to me only, but unto all them also that love his appearing."

The Lord's Supper is "till He come".

And thus that dark betrayal-night
With the last advent we unite,
By one blest chain of loving rite,
Until He come.

So let it be!

Other books by
E. F. Kevan
published by Evangelical Press

OW THAT I AM A
HRISTIAN

istruction for young Christians

ecoming a Christian is just the beginning of a new
ay of life. The new believer needs help to
nderstand and put into practice the basic teaching
the Bible. This book has been written with a
ew to meeting that need.

his is a book which can be confidently placed in
e hands of those who are young in the faith. The
lentiful references to Scripture which it contains
rovide the authority by which the teaching of the
ook can be tested. It will be found invaluable
ither for private study or as a basis for group study
r discussion.

SALVATION

"Salvation is a big word: it is big in the sense that it covers the meaning of many others. To be 'saved' means to be delivered, to be forgiven, to be pardoned, to be redeemed, to be restored, and much more."

With such a grand view of his subject, the author writes in a warm and lively style on man's need of salvation, and God's gracious provision to meet that need through His glorious plan for redeeming sinners.

"What a tremendous subject, so this book demonstrates, is the theme of Salvation! . . . The apostle Paul described the riches of Christ as 'unsearchable', and he exclaimed: 'Oh the depth of the riches both of the wisdom and knowledge of God!', and these are the sort of expressions that come to one's thoughts as one reads this profound exposition of Divine Salvation."

The Harvester

WHAT THE SCRIPTURES TEACH

Bible study is not just a matter of reading books about the Bible, but a diligent searching of the scriptures themselves. This book, which contains brief surveys of the leading Bible doctrines, is lesigned to help in just this way.

The author writes: "The object of this series of studies . . . is not to study God's Word for you but o assist you to study it for yourself. Hence, merely o read the chapters, is to miss their purpose; they re intended for your thoughtful examination, vith the Scriptures."

Iere is an excellent summary of the greatest iblical doctrines. Dr. Kevan's style is both uccinct and profound, and his work will appeal to ll who desire a better understanding of God's Vord.